I0163829

Father of Pearl

Kevin Cawley

Glass Darkly

2012

Copyright © 2012 by Wm Kevin Cawley

ISBN: 978-1-105-88720-8

1

Potatoes in the microwave
at eight p.m. this New Year's Day:
mail to go before I sleep,
pillows to case and rent to pay.

Snoring through fork-holes, punctured spuds
restore my failing appetite:
a whistle of tin, an Irish air.
What bliss! I breathe. I take a bite.

What bills have piled up since I left!
They fill the coffee table. Stacks
of junk mail hunch their backbones, sigh
and hunker down by income tax.

Check by check and taking care
to check and double check the year
(my debts are lovely, dark and deep)
I settle accounts. And fall asleep.

2

A friend's come in from Iowa.
Tendentious deconstructive talk.
A beer for the friend who drove her truck.
The weariness of his bathroom walk.

We sit and watch a TV show
fit audience for an easy feast,
can tell how the old Incredible Hulk
has mellowed in Beauty's friend the Beast.

They keep their distances intact,
sleep well or well enough alone:
chaste Beauty mortared in her tower,
the Beast holed up in low-down stone.

Occasional crises bring them close,
an occasional poem, an occasional dose
or romance tendered at the end.
Then home to bed as friend and friend.

3

Mostly I get mad at me --
boastful in my reticence,
a well-known know-it-all and yet
shallow and short on human sense.

The raging spirit dwelling in
the pages of my diary
admires the likes of Mr. Spock,
wired with logic, trouble-free.

Week by week I make my trek
make tracks across a field of snow
blot by blot divulge myself
the plot behind what all I know

the future of my daily past
a future that could never last --
my history obvious, open and shut.
A mystery, though, why Who done What.

4

Blowing the globe up, out of breath
growing a body based on air
I scare myself with tightening skin
a terrorist in a rocking chair.

A great dictator bouncing up
the fate of millions on his heel
kicked back as if to emphasize
the trickiness of his appeal

elicits love from the Herrenvolk
implicitly embodies them
the manifest of their destiny
their standing orders cut by whim.

Inflated world and rubbery
inflated as the currency --
the Master Race with bated brand
the flaccid made to make a stand.

5

Mas Dios, St. Teresa cried
fastening on the keel of grief,
an anchorite, a barnacle,
a canticle clamoring: No relief.

Mehr Licht! Mehr Licht! as Goethe said
uncertain at the end. More light!
Dimness his inheritance,
fee simple to a plot of night.

After another one by one
we chaff away at grains of grist
thrashing to bare the seed of God
the cache in the kernel always missed.

Not God we say and look for more.
Not God knee deep on the theshing floor.
Not this nor this nor this nor this --
our mystical way the way we miss.

6

February. Expeditions
pebble my soul: impressive grit
I gather makes a good depression,
father of pearl, a perfect fit.

The seminar of a walk to work
tempers my temper. Taking on
fresh irritants every other step
I lash out less, in fact grow fond,

affectionate even, ready to take
the next affront and grow a stone
make rubble a semi-precious plant
double my crop with a cultured clone.

A yield sign in front of me:
I yield to my infirmity.
And by my yield shall you know
the right or wrong of the way I go.

7

And on my walk an obstacle
I ponder almost every day.
It gives me pause to contemplate:
a river of metal in my way.

The mercury's hit bottom now.
I worry my thermometer
may never recover. I fear the wind.
I layer my flesh with plastic fur.

I stand on the bank. The cars flow by
in random patterns, streaming leaves,
colorful gravity boats that gravely
follow what every leaf believes:

the need to have one's own career
the need to rush along, the cheery
formulas, Hello, Goodbye.
Normality ignoring why.

8

I also on the other bank
my pulse improving as I hike
employ the means at my command
rejoice in what I've learned to like.

With second thoughts in back of me
I recklessly approach a first
an Eden where the snow comes down
and Adam forgets what he's rehearsed.

By evening as I travel home
achievements packed in memory
distract me from the ultimate
immaculate anxiety.

Another wait at the one-way road
another chance to weigh my load
and wonder why and see a way
to blunder ahead in the dead of day.

9

Mardi Gras: the year puts on
its carnival of valentines
candied cherries wrapped in foil
dance and patter, borrowed lines.

Greeting cards impressively
repeat whatever we'll pay to swear:
a rented tux conceals the soul's
unmentionable underwear.

At the Brazilian costume ball
Saturday gives up to sun:
they start their Tuesday early there
martyred in agonies of fun.

Funny the agonies don't stop.
Funny how people keep it up
forgetting to go by way of Lent
toward what St. Valentine once meant.

10

Take pity on poor Lucifer,
a citizen, a diplomat,
an angel fond of bargaining,
no stranger to the charm of chat.

Job held up against the worst:
probing made him gripe and wince
but in the end win back again
the plenty of an ever since.

Vanity, all vanity:
but man has a way of passing out
knocked cock-eyed by the new world champ
like Rocky in his title bout.

Out of shape and out of breath:
out for the count, fans; out for death.
Poor Lucifer can't hope to die --
truce after treaty, lie after lie.

11

The Party of God in Lebanon
martyrs its members, hardens hearts,
enables them to spend their rage
on the fabulous wisdom it imparts.

Choice: a righteous right to choose
the voice of Allah: right to kill
defenseless individuals
a constitutional codicil.

Oh, we have terror here as well,
freedom to slaughter, cause to fight:
where personality comes first
murder becomes a person's right.

Meanwhile down in Rio braves
find meaning in torture, kill their wives.
Honor exonerates. Wipe your sword.
An international accord.

12

March. The military months,
starchy outfits, shiny shoes,
personify the businesslike,
admonish us all to pay our dues.

In corduroy jeans, a flannel shirt,
I order my place, assemble files
by rank in time and alphabet
in banks of boxes, miles and miles.

A Chinese puzzle of the past
a blinding maze of trail and shelf
boxes in boxes, aisle after aisle --
intoxicating draft of self.

I map these archives, ins and outs,
a map of the more familiar routes,
index mainly proper nouns,
principal waterways, counties, towns.

13

Invest in wisdom, put it on,
inestimable armor: wear
the weariness experience
makes ears to see by, eyes to hear:

the wariness of discipline,
the very opposite of fun,
a visor made of irony
behind which lips may safely pun.

And always, behind the punning, pain:
the fall of man, banana peel,
the snake that gives the wise the slip
and makes the peanut gallery squeal.

Condoms! the Surgeon General cries.
Condoms alone will make you wise!
In every word the General said
never a hint we end up dead.

14

How odd that classical goods become
our modern evils: *apatheia*
fading into apathy,
mediocritas today

considered mediocrity.
Fitness we go in for now
more an athletic aim to please
with formulas that show us how

to monitor our calories.
But on the other hand old vice
can do the work of virtue. So
enthusiastic now means nice.

Once it meant fanatical.
It once meant full of Spirit, full
of God. You might say born again.
How odd we should admire it then.

15

Woke up dizzy. Staggered to the
clock. Cut the buzzer off
and made the bed. The bathroom. Losing
weight. The kitchen. Brewing coffee.

Butter another muffin? Running
late. Routine took over. Through
the door. What now? What happened to the
car? A boot-high bout of snow.

A foot that kicked the future out.
It put my presence to the test.
The past came back. Too late to walk.
Master the drift. To work at last.

Still dizzy, though. A dizzinessman
still dizzy as the day went on.
Snow pestered the window, spring and all
wrestling winter fall by fall.

16

The tape deck on my closet shelf
stopped one day eight years ago.
The pot I heated water in
gave out say back a month or so.

Sunday on the first of spring
I wondered why it took so long
to toast my cinnamon-raisin bread.
Most of the time when things go wrong

I fiddle a bit with plugs and cords,
kidding around with a mock repair --
unscrew the screws, take off the tops,
do it myself. And stand and stare.

The toast I finally made that day
I toasted with my fiancée:
she broke it off and made us friends.
Spoke up. Said: I prefer the ends.

17

In Ireland a funeral:
the IRA supplies a gun.
The wrath of man makes Protestants
claim Catholics serve the Evil One.

The bishop himself denounced the mob
wishing that Christians wouldn't kill:
two British soldiers beaten, shot,
as witnesses drank in their fill.

Cameras took it down on tape,
samples of a century
in which we lost six million Jews
and Christians looked and didn't see.

This time which will play the Jew?
This time Protestant? Catholic? Who?
Fallacy, prelapsarian lapse.
The Palestinian perhaps.

18

Joshua took Jericho
by squashing citizens. I hear
trumpets and shouting. Walls come down.
I jump to Ruth, surprised by fear.

Fascist orders from the Lord,
the Master of the Universe
recommending genocide
but checking plunder with a curse.

Hitler declared he heard from God
to pit himself against the Jews.
TV preachers pass the Word
revealing God's pro-Contra views.

God has always taken sides:
our God, the God of Genocides,
a real man, a stand-up guy,
no frail Jew to crucify.

19

Good Friday. Also April first.
Dry but cloudy. Chance of rain.
Driving east for Easter, I
arrive with birthday on the brain.

With crocuses in bloom again
some joker calls the radio
raving about the proper plural.
Save the croak-eye. Greek, you know.

Meanwhile women check the tomb,
find it empty, head for town.
False conclusions resurrect
the elsewhere of his settle down.

Not here. A message in the mud.
Not here: another name for God.
I croak, you croak, he-she-it.
We croak. Krokoi: Do Your Bit.

20

The window by my desk at work
makes splendid days look bleak to me:
a milky way between the panes
welcomes the milky way I see.

Eyes that make for life-long fog
try to peer through cloudy glass,
inhale a cloudless afternoon
through veils of vapor, solid gas.

But as the afternoon wears on
by passing down and out the sun
enters the purview of my panes
to interview me one on one.

Blinded by this repartee
blindly I begin to say
I see. Because of course I don't.
But feel *I might* now, not *I won't*.

21

Old Samuel also passed the word,
told Saul to slaughter, slaughter them all.
He lied, killed men, spared animals.
(Why do you persecute me, Saul?)

Killed thousands. David tens of thousands.
Solomon killed only time.
Greatly favored by the Lord
he prayed for wisdom in his prime.

Not wealth not victory not sex.
These followed him by accident:
essential only to relax
into whatever the world had meant.

Vapor, vapor, everything
vapor of vapor lingering:
breath translated *vanity*.
Death of Solomon. End of me.

22

A rosary of resentments: as
she dozes in bed she tells her beads,
ticks off the things that tick her off
plucking them out like garden weeds.

A psychological device
making religion obsolete.
As Cupid to her Psyche once
(how stupid) I agreed to meet.

A marriage of impediments.
Carefully we kept things dark,
shut bushel baskets, loads of light,
put curiosity in park.

But thanks to the lamp of therapy
(thank God) she got the best of me:
they frightened her, peculiar things,
my light, my easy yoke of wings.

23

May day. Polish workers strike.
Mayhem from the IRA.
The Jordan -- still preoccupied.
The Persian Gulf? We're there to stay.

Indiana in the sun
ministers to candidates,
questions their intentions, would-be
presidents of the United States.

Tuesday comes: the cast of votes,
news however obvious,
confirms a general tendency
in terms of mandatory fuss.

Mayday's come to mean distress.
M'aidez. Help! We do our best
and other nations lay the blame
on motherly US who heard and came.

24

Hay-fever season, bad this year.
Leaves and blossoms tangle. Petals
fall in puddles under trees
or maul my window as they settle.

Sunday. Intermittent wind
thunders against my bedroom door.
Petals shredded through the screen
settle on pillows, quilt the floor.

Waking from a sneezy nap
shaken by pentecostal dreams
lungs gone breathless in the gale
tongues descending, tongues of flame,

I open my eyes. And what I see
opens the gash, the dream in me:
rude beauty blazing on the floor,
intruder rattling the door.

An utterance has energy:
muttering to myself I make
a cold apartment warmer, feeling
bolder now, a bit less shaky.

Laundry calls for comment. In a
quandary I address my tub.
To be or not. Et cetera.
To sleep, to dream. I: there's the rub.

Drying sweaters on a rack
mildly euphoric now
I move along to lyric verse.
(I never saw a purple cow.)

Outside I see a purple sky --
outside my window warm and dry
a breeze for pollen and mold to ride.
I sneeze. I mutter. I stay inside.

26

Granted the beds look neater now
planted with ornamental breeds
otherwise covered by chips of bark
to smother the germs of last year's weeds.

Agreed the view has opened up:
no seedling greens to interfere,
my vision of the parking lot
collision-free, pollution clear.

Last year weeds came up unchecked:
casting a forest on the wall
they made my living room a cave
a shady solitude till fall.

Living halfway under ground
I lived in the literally profound --
dominion where potatoes sprout,
where onions plan their coming-out.

27

June. Vacation. On the train
I train myself to fall asleep
bolt upright in a broken coach
coupled to a ruptured seat.

Weariness finds ways to nap --
Erie, Buffalo, Syracuse:
my transmigration of the map
cancels the dark that cancels views.

Morning among the finger lakes:
borne again on rubber wheels
alumni bound for Ithaca
know somewhat how Ulysses feels.

At home no longer in the know.
No Homer to explain it though.
Acquaintances don't recognize
the faint behind a bluff disguise.

Greek to me, a lexicon
for speakers in a foreign tongue:
place names on a college plat
tracing phrases Homer sung.

Attempted continuity
redemption by a scholar's magic
formulas, Aristotelian
norms to qualify the tragic.

Quaint incomprehensible
remainders of those pioneers
who settled here, imported books,
prattled absolutes for years.

A creek erodes their paradise
a creek no scholar steps in twice
with falls to help one contemplate
the call of gravity one calls fate.

29

Still, nostalgia makes no sense
nil nisi bonum misapplied
a snake in love with cast-off skin
mistaken faith. A god has died.

Better break his idol up:
forget how much it looks like you.
Go at it with a hammer, blast it,
scatter its granules. Make it new.

How can anyone suppose
now that god has passed away
he ever had a right to claim
the never-ending final say?

The word at last lets quiet win,
the word that gets the last word in.
An educated listener hears
its edges lopping off both ears.

30

Last night an unexpected frost
frightened gardeners as they slept.
They quivered, pulled their covers up.
(Deliver us from promise kept.)

A man who'd never had a child
had planted no seed and lost no crop
warned off by his clairvoyant wife.
(Aren't you glad I made you stop?)

Thanks to a government subsidy
one anxious farmer rests in peace:
paid to leave his fields untilled
he made a fortune in the freeze.

Zero population growth.
Zero penalty. Best for both
when man and woman, man and wife
make plans to optimize their life.

31

July. An independence day
too dry for fireworks ahead.
Noise I'll never miss. A cultured
oyster home alone in bed,

I'm salivating pearl, making
callousness a work of art --
a secret held by tender flesh,
by cheek that means to check the smart.

Tongue interred in irony --
the young in one another's arms,
dolphins, gong-tormented sea
all whimpering like smoke alarms.

Batteries almost dead. Assaulting
batteries my most grievous fault:
I sabotage that distant gong,
that troubling sea of somethings wrong.

32

When solitude involves a soul,
hollow full of hollow, how
can loneliness solidify?
Only an empty question now.

Appointments having lead to dis-
appointments, as they often do,
alone means loneliness again,
a bone to gnaw, a haunting who.

We used to imitate an owl
by cooing *who*. The sound we made
resembled the cry of a common dove,
the lonesome kind, proverbial breed.

A mourning dove. Or should that be
a morning dove? Orthography
may understand a silent you.
I wonder why. And who. And who.

33

Broccoli I bought for guests
who balked at what I said I'd cook
grows rubbery in the crisper drawer.
It troubles me. I take a look.

Christmas cheese they couldn't eat
sits molding on the shelf above;
yogurt left by someone else
betokens inappropriate love.

Meanwhile in the freezer beans
remain from several months ago,
leftover turkey in plastic bags,
unsafe to eat for all I know.

Why keep it then? Why keep decay?
Why keep the lively disarray
of possibilities gone bad?
Toss it. Bag it. Go with Glad.

34

A party of one, I celebrate
with artful repartee. Belated
comebacks modify a wit
too dumb in company to rate.

Nobody here to disappoint.
I cope with things as they come up.
A word to the waiter: dated cream
has curdled in my coffee cup.

Easily fixed. Polite exchange:
my please and thank-you, his regrets --
a ritual dance of courtesy
admitting guilt, forgiving debts.

Our father Art in heaven knows
the fatherhood he freely chose:
premeditated kids astray
with bread not stone his repartee.

August. Thunder. Days of rain.
My soggy shoes recuperate
dry in the bathtub all night long
and I go barefoot to my fate.

I walk around the neighborhood
talking with my former friend
who now regrets the shower itself
and how the shower had to end.

What does she want? The drought goes on.
The stuttering anecdotes of rain
hardly provide an antidote
on farms of desiccated grain.

Only regrets. RSVP.
Only regrets will answer me.
Impossible to give regret
a rest. Make peace again. Forget.

36

Left alone, I contemplate
the weft of my economy
the warp of my expenditure
the torpor in the weave of me.

Human ecology as they call
home economics at Cornell:
my own devices liven up
the tone of what I have to tell.

Inertia imitating life:
perky as a doll on strings,
I tap my head; I move my lips
with babble fed by hidden springs.

Sublimely unaffected geese
sublimely fly their V of peace:
a ragged banner beckoning,
a flag without a following.

37

Those ducklings our reflecting pool
suckled on bugs all summer long
look almost like their mother now.
Practically grown. Except their song.

A mewling peeping nestling noise
reveals their immaturity --
I heard a flock of smaller birds
the first time it occurred to me.

And for a time I couldn't place
such mournful messages in ducks,
couldn't believe their open bills
wouldn't produce the usual quacks.

Becoming ordinary now,
becoming evidence of how
revision may prove *comme il faut*
for visionaries in the know.

Leaves already on the ground.
Given the drought we've had this year
with many leaves already brown
we can't expect much color here.

Although the grass begins to green
to grow a bit before the freeze
the recent rain will not reverse
a season's damage to the trees.

In Yellowstone the fires burn on,
color, a million shades of flame:
the government chose to let them go,
recover the wilderness, make it tame.

Acres of charcoal clearing left,
acres of drabness; ashes drift,
negative images, anti-snow
figuring fortunes, how they blow.

September. At my sister's wedding
timber formed a crucifix
radiated ceiling beams
their weight and light, their branching sticks

rooted in that central cross
a suitable text for errant eyes
a carpenter's kind of parable
smart in its structural disguise.

No aisle up the middle here:
bride as marginalium.
No statue of the Virgin but
the plaster one she brought from home.

Joined in a church not yet complete
joined to the carpenter's living tree:
the fruit those crafty branches bear
duty free and bound to care.

Blackbirds in our backyard forest,
grackles, starlings pause to talk
soon to make their yearly journey
band together, form one flock.

But here they only perch and chatter
curious company for men
who haven't heard of their migration
every autumn, three as one.

A conversational opener
to conquer the top of a can of ploys:
homecoming weekend coming up --
gambits for graduate girls and boys.

The nature they love they put to use;
nature supports their various views:
good old Mortality! Quietude! Strife!
Football is also a Lot Like Life.

Careworn clothing of the flesh
barely covering the bone:
St. Francis on a sculptor's mind
a man made pertinent in stone.

He called the body Brother Ass --
always a stubborn animal
a legend of rebellious bile
passionate gesture, backward pull.

Yet many confuse him with Friar Tuck
not unattractive but overweight;
among the animals *he* loved most
the ones he piled on his plate.

Not so St. Francis: a skeletal man's
not so full of dinner plans.
No fuss. No budget. Beggary
and trust in Lady Poverty.

42

And Clare, poor Clare, Francesco's friend --
terrifying selfless love --
we'd rather study Abelard
blathering Romance from above.

Looking down on Eloise
he took her over, took her in,
married her opportunities
and buried them in a sense of sin.

Soon as she made her marriage vows
he sent her to a convent: she
a duty now, a body to
repudiate, to set him free.

Promised always to obey,
promised him he'd have his way.
Her family had a way with bulls.
They trimmed away his testicles.

43

October. Snow that doesn't stick:
its sober testament foretells
the consequence of normal growth
which honest entropy impels.

A colorful autumn after all,
a full-blown spectacle: the reds
of sumac, maple, ivy leaves
make mums look sickly in their beds.

Over their unimpressive bloom
covering up an asphalt sky
the canopy of color claims
it *can* be glorious to die.

Joy in sorrow -- mysteries.
Joy in sorrow when the trees
broken by frost release their freight:
an oak leaf on a picnic plate.

44

Weird to think we think of weeds
as worthless yet admire the blight
of ivy on our college walls.
A marvel how we wrong the right.

We slice up babies in the womb
and use them in our medicine,
discover their potential to
improve the health of businessmen.

We tear down shelter in the slums
to spare the eyes of passers-by:
we make the homeless move along:
we take their place: we gentrify.

The law declares we have the right:
the law has teeth; the law can bite.
We hold these truths self-evident.
We mold the clay of what they meant.

45

The flesh, the tongue inside the shell,
the fish behind the barricade,
the part with taste has truth to tell,
artfully rounded, hard, well-made.

This bead, this bit of bitterness
the breeder means to take away,
will string along with others, just
a thing of substance on display.

"Oh oysters come and walk with us,"
the voice of so-called culture cried:
the flesh can't fence away its thrust,
its passion for the pearl inside.

Made flesh give out, give up the word --
made flesh turn meat before, I've heard:
as many times as word made flesh
the hangman strung and hung the catch.

46

Stairwell: nowhere on the way to
nowhere else, a land of landings
neutral places in between
those outings where I make a stand.

Timeless: neither up nor down
a sameness in it either way
no windows to admit the world
noon all night or midnight day.

A commonwealth of banisters:
seemingly there to stop a fall
they benefit the suicide
that winters in this upright hall.

Well of echoes from below:
well above a trace of snow
powders the cake-like exit shack
doubts my designs and turns me back.

47

November. Snow in earnest now.
Remember? Inches over night.
We run to open curtains leaking
unacceptable delight.

We have no walk to shovel off
no driveway to put right again
no parents in the neighborhood.
No marriage makes us act like men.

No *no*. The two of us go out
and throw some snowballs in the pond
reach for branches, bones of trees.
Free to wander and respond.

We ponder possibilities
ponder the discipline that frees:
responsible in our response
we want what every child wants.

48

Clear weather seems to clear my head:
the bleariness outside this morning
warns me of the coming storm;
a storm inside confirms the warning.

I want what every child wants.
I wonder what I meant by that.
I haunt myself, my childhood haunts,
a sinus headache in a hat.

A thunderhead obliterates
the wonder of a day of snow,
reduces to adulthood my
illusion of an all to know.

Elections over: death goes on
electing: votes for everyone:
an absolute majority:
a habit of democracy.

49

Thanksgiving. Artificial thanks
delivered by Uriah Heep
rise from a hundred million homes,
eyes unctuous and half asleep.

We put the wilderness on hold:
goodness called for husbandry.
By cranking nature into goods
we sanctified economy.

Still, we wanted nature too.
The wilderness gave up on us.
We get a busy signal now.
We set our teeth and take the loss.

Teeth made out of porcelain,
teeth perfected, need to grin
prefiguring in gratitude
the rigor mortis brought by food.

50

The sculptor Ivan Mestrovic
had hoped to make a cross for God
that bore in front in high relief
the corpus of the crucified

and on the spine, the other side,
a monstrance of the risen Christ,
the tomb unsealed, the rock rolled back,
the groom arriving at the feast.

But men with money to dispense
have many notions of their own.
Why so big? Why carve the back?
Why did he have to work in stone?

And who would go around behind?
Who would explain the scene they'd find?
And wouldn't he make the corpse less grim?
They couldn't bear to look at him.

51

December. My insomnia
with cymbals trembling lets me know
that intellect cannot command
the brain to stop its stop-and-go.

The woman of my wakefulness,
the same who said goodbye last March
hello again last August, lately
fell in love with me in church.

It happened half a month ago.
Her rapture now has given way
to one more ultimate goodbye.
Her final word came yesterday

and met her other final words
met in my headroom, buffalo herds
percussion enough to shake the ground
with dust to dust and round and round.

52

So what can I look forward to?
Another season on the run,
the press of Christmas shopping, then
depression in the wake of fun.

Whose will have I been praying on?
The military me at prayer:
my kingdom come, my will be done
my thing my own my only care.

Advent. What a stubborn child!
Hundreds of years ago the wise
debunked him, stripped him, nailed him down.
He's back, and in the same disguise.

As if we couldn't see him through
as if -- but we have work to do
presents to buy and cards to sign
and pleasant fits of me and mine.

53

One might suppose the animals
would shy away from human trails
test the oddly stunted tracks
pause to nose them, smell the smells.

The rabbit I imagine here
inhabiting this patch of trees
would vanish in the undergrowth
renounce the human dream of ease.

A path made broad by traffic, flat
by athletes on their morning run
made white by freshly fallen snow --
and I arrive before the sun

to walk it in my gum-soled shoes
to walk to work, the same old news.
But look! Fresh tracks of rabbit show
one took the way I mean to go.

54

My VCR a bathysphere
to see the deep, the late at night --
daytime doesn't interest me
games and soaps and talk-show hype.

I've seen it on my sick days home.
I mean to plumb a mystery
deeper than a midnight host
creepy beyond a vampire feast.

What pale, what eyeless fish I find!
What millionaires who want to sell
the secret of success so I
may seek its benefits as well!

The gospel of the foolproof plan
the gospel of the Rich Young Man:
sell yourself and follow me.
The wealth you dwell on sets you free.

55

New Year's Eve. The Beast remains;
Beauty has not been canceled yet.
Terror dominates the news --
airline bombing, hundreds dead.

By shortwave radio the world
importantly elucidates
the latest scandal of success,
weighs its death-toll, how it rates.

Amateurs informally
tramp the same well-trampled ground,
quote the broadcast views of pros
with no quotation marks around.

I listen as I pay my bills.
I listen to a million wills
their lasting testament of trials
their history of codicils.

www.ingramcontent.com/pod-product-compliance
Lightning Source LLC
Chambersburg PA
CBHW020524030426
42337CB00011B/542